T0113347

THE CHRISTMAS SHOW

BARNARD NEW WOMEN POETS SERIES

Edited by Christopher Baswell and Celeste Schenck

THE CHRISTMAS SHOW

HARRIET LEVIN

With an Introduction by Eavan Boland

BEACON PRESS

Boston

Beacon Press
25 Beacon Street
Boston, Massachusetts 02108-2892
www.beacon.org

Beacon Press books
are published under the auspices of
the Unitarian Universalist Association of Congregations.

© 1997 by Harriet Levin
All rights reserved

First digital-print edition 2001

Library of Congress Cataloging-in-Publication Data
Levin, Harriet
The Christmas show / Harriet Levin ; with an introduction by Eavan Boland.
p.   cm.
ISBN 0-8070-6837-3 (pbk.)
I. Title.
PS3562.E88959C48   1997
811'.54—dc20   96-35462

for my mother, my father, Fran, and Cheryl
—and for Rick

CONTENTS

ACKNOWLEDGMENTS

Grateful acknowledgment is given to the following publications, in which some of these poems first appeared:

"Thrown Out" in *The Iowa Review*; "In Grandfather's Stamp Room" in *New Letters*; "Sustenance" in *Nimrod* (winner of the Pablo Neruda Prize); "The Christmas Show" in *The Partisan Review*; "What Stopped Her" in *West Branch*. "The Christmas Show," "I Begin to Leave Home When I Read Darwin," "Father's Hut in the Sedan," and "There's Something to Be Said" received the Grolier Poetry Prize from the Ellen LaForge Memorial Poetry Foundation.

I wish to thank the Poetry Society of America for the honor of its Alice Fay di Castagnola Award for this manuscript-in-progress. And my thanks to New York State Poets in Public Service, The Corporation of Yaddo, and The Virginia Center for the Arts, without whose gifts of time and space these poems could never have been written.

I am indebted to Eavan Boland, Chris Baswell, Marya Van't Hul, Jill Bialosky, and Cheryl Sucher for their help with this book.

INTRODUCTION

The very first poem in this book is the title poem. It is called "The
Christmas Show." Immediately—this happens with other poems
here as well—the reader senses that something is wrong. It is like
being stopped by a friend whose voice is everyday and ordinary, in
which we are used to hearing all kinds of dear and absorbing daily-
ness, and realizing that the tone is different. And realizing, also,
that the voice, and our sense of it, is altered by this tone. That, in
fact, it has been so fractured by the news it brings that the small
comforts of the world which were once its customary narrative will
never be the same again:

> While my youngest sister lies
> on a cold cellar floor
> in a house whose broken windows hold back nothing
> and three boys pin down her shoulders
> and force their way past her belt buckle, I am watching
> The Christmas Show at Radio City Music Hall, seeing
> a full moon accentuate the otherworldliness
> of children dressed as elves, skating snowmen
> and cardboard reindeer.

Harriet Levin is a wonderfully courageous and exacting
poet. Her care for her themes—dark as some of them are—is
equaled by a rigorous attention to a poem's shape, to the sharpness
of a line break or the accuracy of a cadence. She is also a beautiful
lyricist. It may be strange to argue that beauty as well as distinction
is the effect of this poem, but it is. "The Christmas Show," like
other poems in this book, insists on a world where contraries exist:
The young girl is violated in the very society which is trying out its

legend of innocence in a festive show. In this way, the loneliness of
sexual violence is allowed to comment on that other construct
which all societies hide behind: the myth of inviolable childhood.

And yet the beauty does not come from these unswerving
oppositions. It emerges from the poet's voice—out of a music
whose source is the narrator's openness to the dangers she evokes.
There is no ornament here, and no false rhetoric. There is just that
dark melody of the poet saying to us, how will we ever know the
truth if we put our language in the service of an opposite fiction?
And suddenly the poem opens out into a heartbreaking and con-
cerned argument about the ethics and limits of expression. And
through it all we hear the poet whispering, *who am I? What should
I do?* And the poem becomes beautiful in inverse proportion to the
answerability of these questions.

Many more of the poems here have that mix of candor and
engagement. The candor acts as a catalyst for a lyric dissonance
that emerges in all kinds of surprising places, offering unexpected
views. "Buoyancy," to take just one example, has an exuberant,
spiraling syntax. The lines spin away into a wonderful snapshot of
"the splash / of my entire class jumping into the pool / one night,
sweaty from dancing." You read the poem. You stand back. You
ask yourself, with a kind of wonder, now where was that? What
particular night of noise, moonlight, laughter, truancy, teenage
spirits lasted long enough to make this poem? To justify that bold
first line: "I want to see the whole world at once, like the splash."

Asking this question, and re-reading poems like "The
Christmas Show" and "Buoyancy," I feel confirmed in my sense
that a new poetry is being written by women in America—a poetry
which this distinguished competition has done so much to foster.

xii

t is not an easy set of perceptions to be exact about, and yet reading Harriet Levin's work evokes this newness so powerfully that it seems worth trying to define it here.

There seems to me—I say this with both the diffidence of an outsider and the enthusiasm of a reader—a new generation of American women poets, perhaps in their late thirties, allowing some years on either side. When I read their poems I see that they tried out their first lipsticks, had their first sexual experiences, wrote their first poems against a backdrop of space exploration, in the aftermath of the Vietnam War, and to the noise of household gods falling. Unlike my generation in Ireland, they had read Plath, Bishop, and Rich by the time they knew they were poets. Their poems avail easily of the lyric and narrative distinctions which have been so much a part of the vocabulary of American poetry since the Second World War. And, almost without seeking it out, they become—as Harriet Levin certainly is—compelling political poets. They tell the story of their nation through the lens of their sexuality. To their generation has come that rare and costly poetic gift: the erotics of history. If this seems a narrow prescription, then it is a narrowness that reaches out to include Horace and Whitman as well as Adrienne Rich.

Harriet Levin's poems will attract many readers. They will recognize their world in her cadences: the urban darknesses, the family quarrels, the trips across oceans and continents that end up in a new engagement with the American poem. But they will also have the chance to listen for something different. And this difference is in the way she, as a poet, sees the world: With care and accuracy. With anger and music. Without any loss of faith—and this is demonstrated by the beautiful, terrible strength of the title poem—that poetry and silence retain the capacity to learn from one another.

Finally, I want to say that it has been a privilege to read and judge this and the other manuscripts in this group. It is through such contests, and through the voices which they announce, that contemporary poetry receives a necessary sustenance. I am grateful to have been part of the process. For that I have to thank Chris Baswell for his grace, and for the friendship he brings to poets and poetry. I also want to thank Donna Masini, whose poetry I admire, and whose counsel and help has been invaluable.

Eavan Boland

1

The perception of women in our civilization is at a fundamental
level also the perception of the world. This is part of the truth
which rape expresses. That a man is alienated from a woman and
does violence to her reflects the essential condition underlying this
civilization. The one is alienated from the other. I am alienated
from you. One nation is alienated from another. What is human is
alienated from nature, from the universe.

– Susan Griffin

Rape: The Politics of Consciousness

THE CHRISTMAS SHOW

While my youngest sister lies
on a cold cellar floor
in a house whose broken windows hold back nothing
and three boys pin down her shoulders
and force their way past her belt buckle, I am watching
The Christmas Show at Radio City Music Hall, seeing
a full moon accentuate the otherworldliness
of children dressed as elves, skating snowmen
and cardboard reindeer.
While my youngest sister lies on her back, stripped naked,
and three boys, one at a time, move over her, I am applauding
when an entire row of girls
wearing bright red bathing suits
fleeced with white fur
kick open their legs, the whole house applauds
at that moment. While my youngest sister looks into the dark
wide pupils she will look into
for the rest of her life, the boys
who prick her throat with a knife
feel only a momentary pleasure.
And just when I think The Christmas Show is over,
the curtain opens once more
with sheep, straw and stars
and the story of the nativity begins,
of a birth with no sex in it.
A real live camel is led across the stage
in a caravan with sheiks, children, and beggars

waiting to be touched and saved,
but at that moment
my mother is rushing to open the front door
my sister pounds
and pounds on, blood on her face, her lips
swollen, her cheek swollen, her
eyes swollen, having seen enough.

BEGIN TO LEAVE HOME
WHEN I READ DARWIN

imagine myself raging
in the world outside my head, the sequoia,
my Father of the Forest, lying prostrate
in Calaveras Grove, *Its heart eaten by fire*

and its huge limbs consumed. Here, in the Andes,
with leaves, pine cones, condors, giddiness prevails.
Once in ten thousand years a woman meets a man
like Manuel. He gives me black silk veils.

When sweat beads my forehead, the bed a ship,
and I'm drifting past *skeletons of Indians hanging
from trees breast-high with giant thistle,*
timber and mud where Conception stood,

burrowed into the earth like an armadillo
screaming, feeding on the sores on horses' backs,
Manuel comes and takes my hand. He does not let go.
We tango in a cool marble hall on a cool

marble floor, the orchestra a flight of tanagers,
rock-still. When Father's ill
we wind his head in a compress of split beans.
We leech his blood with tiny worms

Manuel pries from the bromelia. Father wants us
near him. We ask if we disturb his sleep. He says, "Oh, no!"
White petrified pines rise outside my window,
These trees once stood on the Atlantic Shore, now 77 miles away.

They sunk beneath the sea then rose 700 feet.
When I see them I understand tenacity.
Its anchor embedded deeply. Sickness is not in my sisters' heads.
Argentina is not their dream nor Manuel their man.

The lines on their palms are not a jagged precipice
where childhood stands. They watch television
on the flowered couch, Father between them.
They feel loved enough.

THE MAGNITUDE OF THE CRISIS

Making a list of clothes to pack for the beach
on an already frothy day of arguments
and more arguments, I open a file,
innocuously marked, "rape1" and find

thin humus on the ground, my sister's letter:
Dear Rapists, I feel like you're still following me.
Everyone I come in contact with
is you. Who do you think you are? Live your

life and let me live mine! I hate you! Fuck
you! Go away you fucking assholes! Fuck you!
I despair over how, two decades later
her image in that mirror cannot be cut

and burned. My husband is yelling at me
for packing too many suitcases
our last vacation, one big one just books.
I despair over the trauma she must

carry along, finally seeing why
when we asked her if she wanted to go to the beach
with us, she raised her arms despairingly,
arms already weighted down. I am thinking

how the very concept of a beach in summer,
the unfiltered light, the roughness of sand
smears itself all over her body.
In half an hour, if not less,

I can reduce all my excess
baggage into one burgeoning. But this
is how my life is different from my sister's,
I have not been forced to struggle for it.

FATHER'S SHUT IN THE SEDAN

Halfway home the engine dies. We coast
to a stop, the bushes meshed with cocoons,
life in limbo Molly's barking at.
Father's shut in the sedan. The mountains
are ridged with pines and smoke.
I throw Molly a branch, holly berry
streaked with mud, and walk the cow pasture
thinking about Alan tiptoeing
to unmask the canvas he's done of me.
We lay in the cane chair: shirtless,
smoking Camels, making jokes, listening
to the wind rise and swoon. But the only voice
calling me is Father's, the car revving up
and Molly barking. A yellow finch shows
its wings, the birches their leaves, but nothing
matters to my father. I know the chill
coming out of sleep into gauzy darkness
that follows him. It is the chill I felt
and still feel shut in the memory
of my mother rubbing her legs with suntan oil
and turning to my father to say something
I can't hear or judge. He slaps her hard
across the mouth. I see the stain in the earth.
I hear the car engine stall like betrayal
then father push open the door and plow
through dew-wet grass to check under the hood.
Why has he waited this long to get out

9

of the car?, the engine moaning in his throat.
It dies, moans, dies. Cows huddle. Turkey hawks
corkscrew upward. We ride these roads with nothing
else to do except desire, the stopped wheel
in our hands.

THERE IS SOMETHING TO BE SAID

There is something to be said
for doing what someone else wants
you to do, not the wants of parents
exactly, not my father saying,
I knew you'd decide to do what's right,
not that objective thing he is tugging
at his hair for, seizing a strand
by its roots, feeling clearly
where it begins and ends, not that
ordered conception of life, where what
I am talking about is always wrong,
but meeting someone new, looking straight
at him, his eyes, his mouth,
hearing him say, I want you,
just right away, before we have even talked
and without thinking to botch it up,
saying, yes. Then, I follow him outside
actually walking out
the very door I have been watching
opening back and forth
the way I want to get past myself,
past my own thinking,
to the physical world
where I am stripped naked, feeling
the crushed grass against my skin,
then rising, dressing myself and coming back in,
free of the weight.

BAY OF FUNDY

I remember holding
binoculars to my eyes,
my hunger to witness
something large, and the lighthouse
keeper's wife telling us
whales come here in the winter
keep to the cold—so much
so, they're sighted at a distance
in the desolate air
of snow and you taking back
from me your binoculars saying
simply,—no, extravagantly,
we'll come back in December
just to see them
as if you could yourself control
the sky and the tides
and I wondered how we would travel
off-season, no ferries, only
highway, making time, feeling
as if we had some work
to do and snow so cold
should you bend down to touch
it, your hand would burn.

RACETRACK

in memory of J.L.

The day grandfather took me with him
to the racetrack
grandmother lay propped up in bed,
painted like a mannequin,
a towel draped across her chest.
After my blown kiss, he closes the bedroom door,
his cigarette working its rocky path.
I follow his slow limp to the car.

I had expected Hempstead Plains
or the Aqueduct,
floodlit and glamorous,
and got Liberty Bell Racetrack,
free admission to senior citizens.
No silver trophy. No pinto draped with roses.
No widow wreathed in furs
posed astride her stallion.
No chariot racing up to the clouds with the boy Icarus
and his father.

On a back-row bench, half-deaf,
ear to the loudspeaker's trajectory,
my grandfather marks his tally sheet,
three hundred dollars down on "Dressed Pretty."
He elbows the man beside him,
someone else's grandfather

13

home on disability,
unshaven, collarless,
sporting a pencil stub between his teeth.
In the distance, its powdered gold
ripped open from the earth,
glittering, alert,
the track goes round and round.

I walk to the hotdog stand.
The clubhouse is smoky.
No counter is low enough to lean over.
Everyone here is wearing suspenders,
wiping his nose with a handkerchief,
waving tout sheets like the funeral home advertisements
we use at church as fans.
The trumpets blare like judgment.
The clubhouse clears out.

Is this where it all began
my straining to see
what is kept from me?
I stretch on tiptoes
looking for "Dressed Pretty" in the lead
listening for her neighing
more coy than shrill.

Grandfather, why didn't you lift me onto your shoulders,
point to the red carpet rolled out,
the rush of hooves pounding with our breath,
the gripped rein
rattling in our hands
the way love rushes headlong?
Instead I poked him with an elbow,
my Coke spotting his trousers
just as the crowd rose
to moan
for a horse knocked to its knees,
another buckling under
and a third, "Dressed Pretty"
the loudspeaker trembles,
falling with her legs folded under,
quivering on the turning earth.

His staring soundless,
the sundae he treats me to
chills my throat.
When he drops me off,
he does not promise to take me with him again.
His black sedan circles our cul-de-sac,
then speeds ahead
and does not stop.

BUOYANCY

I want to see the whole world at once, like the splash
of my entire class jumping into the pool
one night, sweaty from dancing. The night air buzzes
with locusts. The quiet lap of water against my body.
It's like swimming in a bath with the full moon
over my head instead of my mother
calling my name behind the locked door, the bathroom steamy,
my face lost in the mirror. The water is too dark
to be murky. The view outside the pool is chairs,
chaises, inner tubes, rubber floats.
Shadows tear up the grass, widen and lengthen.
I start swimming faster, outdistance the others,
stop feeling the connection between their voices
and faces. The world keeps itself from us.
Our class stages a relay, chooses sides,
lines up. We swim faster, shout louder
and louder until everyone's touched finish,
the wall we call finish. (Seeing the whole world at once.)

We climb out of the pool, huddle in blankets,
shivering in the cold.

LIGHT

My daughter is studying
        flight, in school.
She has drawn a time line
        from Icarus
to the Montgolfiers' balloon
        to W. W. II.
How has she come so far
        when I am
suppressed, being entirely
        contained
by the orbit I have been reared in?

Yesterday afternoon, as I was walking
        alone, over
the bridge to her school, the river,
        ducks and quay
inching into their shadows, I turned
        to observe
the flight of a bird, whose flying
        could have led
directly to a truth, when I noticed
        a man
with a black mask on his face,
        not a butterfly's

mask, not a face that had arisen
over time
into a disguise both ephemeral
and beautiful,
hurrying to follow me. I panicked
and ran
kept on running over the bridge's hump,
then downhill,
dipping out of his sight, right through
the intersection,
chancing a more certain injury
then being trapped

at the corner with him. At fourteen,
I narrowly outdistanced
the man who stepped out from behind me
offering to help
when my bicycle lock jammed,
up in the woods,
rain nearly all week, and lightning
thrashing down.
He was bare-chested, his denim shorts rolled
into a cuff
above his knee. Still holding my bicycle chain,
he asked

f I would do *him* a favor,
over there
where groundcover cushions
the earth,
no one else around
to watch,
my bicycle unable to grow wings
in the open air.

Before I got up the courage
to let go
of my daughter's bicycle seat, I imagined her
pedaling on her own

or a brief moment, then I imagined
watching her fly
over the handlebars. Yet what happened
was like nothing
had gathered in my mind. At first, wobbly,
she suddenly sprang upright
soaring beyond grass, houses, trees,
her back to me.
Another time, late to meet friends,
I hitched a ride.
The pony-tailed driver
leaned out

the rolled-down window

    of his pickup,

sweetly sighed, *Oh, a mysterious wind tapped at my door*

    and blew me here!

Even the goldenrod

    on the roadway island

drifted over its borders. After I closed the door

    I saw the beer

in his hand. He asked if I was wearing

    pantyhose.

The car slowed and in the stoplight's

    illuminated lane,

I invoked my parents' names

    praying

one of them would hear,

    breathe into

his ear the something that did

    suddenly spook him

when I said I wanted to get out.

    He leaned over me

to open the door, and I broke away

    as he shouted,

Look out girl! One day you're gonna get screwed

    real bad!

Down to the subway. Where are the sacred stones,
        the worn mosaics
of an earlier era? Vines? A widening trail? Palms?
        All these are missing
as the world shrinks to the gash of light
        ravaging the crack
where a car door opens, the tiniest of openings
        I cannot now slip through.

BIRD OF PARADISE

Orange and purple fanning outward
like the bandanna around the head
of my sister, a fevered span
traversed in the clink
of two glasses. She drinks gin from each,
pinning a skirt in the mirror,
measuring the distance,
the remorse, because
she is always coming back
as someone else.
We think she has come home to us,
bird of paradise, finally driven out
from her world of drugs and pain
where the ground slopes
unevenly, and no word is true enough
to follow mile after mile.
The night she came home
she called me outside
with a handful of stones
against my window,
her red hair aglow.
I watched as she staggered behind the garage,
holding her stomach,
rolling from side to side on the grass.
And each time we bend down

o lift her up

he hurts us,

ier bruised arms,

ınable to feel a thing,

ixed around my father's neck.

VIOLATIVE

Slicing my finger with a knife
cutting ginger for dinner
is not so bad after all,
as having to tell you

your new racing bike got stolen
the day before the triathlon.
I see your face, feel
its feeling of having been bitten

by a hundred mosquitoes.
Then the serpentine questioning,
the swerving from lane to lane,
as you ask who left the house last,

and finally accusing me
of forgetting to close the door
to the garage. But racing has won you medals,
and in love,

your lead prefigures danger,
the curving road,
even the historic markings
where battles were waged

n harshest winter.
Ever since I was a child
and the consequences
of something I had done

were pointed out to me—hitting or taking a toy
from one of my sisters—
have not believed that my act
and its punishment were related.

n my mind, father was the one
pulling me down off the edge
of the pool, or into the fire,
judging the risk,

thinking I would never learn
if he did not show me.
Where, oh where is that place
where consequences have no name,

and when something happens
it is not said to be caused
by me or anyone? Imagine
now a small child

standing on a pier
would point to a fire
someone's lit in an oil drum
on the deck of ship

docked beneath him,

and, endlessly curious, would begin

to lean over right there.

It's at that moment the fire looks

so beautiful, you think it is the origin

of joy, the brightness

(O flickering world!)

that consumes us.

SOME COMFORT IN A HUNTER'S CABIN

At the tollbooth, Father's change
on the dashboard changing hands, he turns
to face me in the backseat of the car
and orders me to, *Sit still, sister.*

I haven't done anything wrong,
but I'm glad he's checked his anger,
hemlocks rooted to the periphery
and the sky rushing into a black fault.

And so, seeking to defend myself
against Father's coldness, I pretend
I am a hunter in the woods
building a cabin bare with extremity:

the table set with tin, the chairs mere crates
and the floor knuckled with iron ore.
From inside I smile and begin to describe
how I cornered a buck, the sole hunter

to have noticed antlers camouflaged in tree branches,
while Father leans back
on his crate, his pipe smoke curled
like an embryo. *I didn't shoot*

the buck, I say. *I turned back first*
having met its gaze, something as startling
as a dream interrupting your talk.
Legs shifting suddenly, father walks to his bed,

which is only a narrow cot, too small
for tossing posed in nightmare.
His bounty under the mattress, a jeweled hunting cap.
He says, *You deserve this now. Wear it proudly.*

You are my only daughter. Then, as if I had truly
pulled a sword out of stone,
I am given the task of keeping the fire sturdy.
It opens blushing.

2

speak to him and he does not answer. Responding to me is the
typical and essential act by which I perceive that I exist for my
fellow man. Now he does not answer me: I have ceased to exist
for him. Now I am not in company with him any longer. And
I discover with a shiver that so far as he is concerned, I am left
alone.

—Ortega y Gasset
Man and Crisis

LOOKING AT THE TEMPLE OF DENDUR

for Katherine Johnson

I gave the assignment: describe anyone
dead or alive in the entire museum
with whom you identify and why.
It was an idea I was working toward:
Does the world lie outside us?
If it is real, can we see it?
Can there be no such thing as opposites?
What attracts us to another person?

I opened the doors to the study of Ramses.
They were heavy like subway doors.
Inside lay the enbalmed bodies,
carved sarcophagi, tombs
painted blue and gold. I was living inside
the bitterness of our last words,
grieving and lonely, when I saw the head
of the Enchantress of Tiye.

She was called the Enchantress,
but no part of her body survived,
nothing to show her sex
except one bronze earring
no one had ever unclasped,
her flesh wholly imaginary.

Like a crown of sunsets, the top of her head was orange.
"Henna-stained" the plaque read

when I read it. In the next case:
linen, brushes, resin.
Not a single preparation missing.
I reach for you, reconstructing
everything as it was.

I touch your hair, black and curly
as any Egyptian's. On the table are roses
you brought to make up for some wrong.
I see their stems through the glass,
seeing right through it. Looking more deeply,
I hear you say you want us to stop
making love. It gives you no joy.
You are turned toward the wall,
the way the guard keeping watch over Ramses' tomb
guards a death that is also his,
even when he walks out the doors
into glistening sunlight.

I'm deciding to not ever talk with you again
when Leroy hands me his paper, his face
as clear as the sky through tree branches:
As I was looking at the Temple and the
other exhibits, I saw a young boy
with his father, taking everything in.
He asked lots of questions about everything.
Where did this piece come from?
How old is it? Did it take long to build?
Is it real? I identify with this young boy
because it is my first time in a museum
and I want to see and know about everything.

I've read Leroy's journal.
His first writing in fifteen years.
Every page marked, *Don't show this to anyone!*
I think of his pen as tongs
he holds to the hot coals
burning inside him and filling him with pain.
You ask me to take off my clothes.
All you want to do is look
at my body. Not touch it.
You are looking at me but thinking

I am someone else, as if sunlight
were hurting your eyes. Someone hands me a batch of papers.
The one on top, Miriam's, reads:
This is a carving of an anonymous woman's face.
Her hair black and thick like mine.
Her eyes looking out at you, like the sea
carrying you to it. I identify with her anonymity.
This is a feature in myself I would not change.
I watch Miriam leaf through her notebook.
Most of the pages empty. Just standing there.
She has survived this way.

Your bicycle's chained to a telephone pole,
the mercury lock pulled through the spokes.
We sit on the hard steps of the stoop.
When I offer you a cigarette you bend
to my cupped hands. Smoke rises
between us, issue of breath.
But it dissolves and disburses.

And later, our bodies bared,
the fan throwing my hair across
your chest, attempting
to reassure me. The parched air
of the museum suddenly lifts
when the small breeze of Katherine's paper
passes from her hand to mine: *When Gregory*

as first missing and found drowned
n the Hudson River, I thought my whole life
ould end. I felt there wasn't any life
ft for me at all. I felt as if I was locked away
n a tomb, that someone had locked me in.
itting here, looking at The Temple of Dendur
nd reading the history of why it was built
akes me think of Gregory. The Temple was built
y the Emperor Augustus shortly after
5 B.C. It was built to bury
is two sons, brothers, who had drowned in the Nile.

ut myself! I had no Temple with enclosed
alls and wharf to hide in. I had no money
o preserve my son's memory. I cannot build
monument to Gregory. I can only preserve
is memory in my mind. Katherine watches me
eading her paper, wanting to know
if she has expressed herself clearly,
anting my face to show it
ke granite carved
ith scenes and texts of the Afterlife,
Iephthys and Isis mourning the dead,
earing a jackal's head and a ram's.

You did what you wanted to,
you flew across the Atlantic.
You looked down at the indistinguishable
fish and shells. I walk toward Katherine,
take her arm. We are figures in a bas-relief
thinking ourselves into a world
the dead inhabit. In my mind I seduce you
wearing the face of someone you once loved.

Leroy stands behind us.
I ask Katherine if he can read her paper.
All semester the class shared their work,
correcting mistakes, they make it seem more real.
I tell Katherine about the Museum Shop
were we can buy postcards of the Temple.
We walk down the wide marble stairs
we climbed to come here.

STILL MOMENT NEAR TIPTON

As we pull off the road the dust
rises into low clouds, dust so
easily stirred. Black Angus watering
at a trough lift their heads, then drift
toward the fence. Their fur
looks ridged with lines a child's finger
cut in sand. With the shifting
of a limb or a tide the lines are destroyed.

You keep to your side of the car
and poke an elbow out the window.
What accusation are you rehearsing?
Drunkenness to the core or
unconscious spite. The fields are tilled
singly with wheat. Tight-lipped,
I focus on the rusted wing of a tractor.

We abuse one another.
I want to edge toward you and touch
my nose to your nose, my mouth
to our mouth, but do not. Your hand lingers
on the ignition. You are reluctant
to start up the car and emerge
from your deep flux of anger to drive
with me past the drowsy cattle
and the low-ranged bluffs bristled
with prairie grass and desultory towns.

37

AMULET

From such slips of the tongue

eyes take fire

Anna Akhmatova

I am coming back
as I said I would
with the grains of sand
from Georgeoupolis in my backpack,
a token of vulnerability,
a few glittering specks
from the erosion
or curses
against love.

What gift would I have
brought back then:
a shetland sweater?
a black beret?
Your voice faltered
then laughing
asked for a vial of sand
from a beach in Crete.
I was traveling as far as Naples
and you had me crossing the Adriatic
without promising love or commitment
without urging
my quick return.

38

I am moving toward you
despite the flashing signal,
though I believe in outward signs.
I believe my ferry
to Athens was canceled
for good reason.
I believe the fungus
infecting my foot
poisoned my bloodstream
for good reason.
I believe the hospital in Brindisi
detained me another day,
another week, all
for good reason.

We are nearing the Swiss border,
passing people, towns, and mountains
the berth-light obscures.
I've boarded the train with my right foot first,
the sore one, accustomed
to pain, stronger for the injury
it insists on sharing,
as I insist on this confrontation
in a language I've reserved
all this time
traveling in foreign countries,
speaking tongues that mean little to me,
words I practiced
in your presence, words

39

with casual meanings,
until I traveled to the place
you sent me, quite by chance,
and saw the sky bearing down
on the sea with deep insistence
quite by chance,
the place where your laughing sent me.

MIDDAY

Last night all I wanted to do,
            tearing off
                        all the moth-eaten leaves
from the lamb's ears in my garden,
            arranging all my books
                        in alphabetical order,
refolding all my winter sweaters,
            was to call
                        and tell you
that I feel I am living half my life in secret,
            that there are lies
                        and evasions
I am unwilling to violate.
            Years ago,
                        when I worked as a waitress
at a diner on Locust Street,
            besides the boss,
                        Manolis,
rather conspicuously trying to rub
            his arm across my breasts
                        whenever he came near,
            I remember
there were a lot of people
            who would just come in alone
                        to be alone.

They would order food and not eat it,
　　leave a big tip
　　　　out of gratitude.
By midday the arc of frost
　　flung across this window
　　　　will have melted.
The other window is clear.
　　You must hold off passing judgment
　　　　on me until you've considered
　　each side.
How can you know it
　　if half is kept secret?
　　　　I want to tell you
that there are days I remember
　　not remembering you
　　　　at all,
nothing so kind as our hands joining
　　in forgiveness,
　　　　after a slip of the tongue,
some words you should hear.

THIS MORNING I WENT AS FAR

This morning I went as far as the cemetery
picking roadside flowers,
coltsfoot, yarrow, wild elderberry,
when the rain started
at first gentle then hard.

Feeling it strike my skin
I remembered your words,
something's bound to happen,
as if the sky over us
were always blackening with clouds
about to break.

It did. You wanted something to happen.
You wanted the rain
to hit your skin hard,
soak through your clothes,
your body, bring you out of it.
You wanted to stand
dripping on the carpet.

Why didn't you leave
the letter Susan wrote outside,
the words, the stamp?
Why did you bring it in?
She said she was flying back,
heartsick with longing.

43

She dreamed of you
sipping anise at her uncle's villa,
the sun at its apex.
Did she think you had already chosen her?
Your backpack on your shoulders.

The rain hit my skin hard.
No boarded-up barns, houses, or sheds.
I was oddly receptive
and so I ran gripping the flowers in my hand,
the way you gripped Susan's letter,
the curtains moving in the wind,
night coming in.

Less than halfway home,
I slipped on the gravel road.
Relinquishing myself as rain does,
I remembered waking to your kiss,
thinking you had left for good.
Instead you came back
only to leave again.
The door slams.
Headlights circle the room,
near, then far from me.

was running faster
isking a fall on the gravel.
There was nowhere to stand out of the rain.
You wanted something to happen and it did.
You wanted to feel
he rain hit hard,
oak through your clothes,
our body, bring the outside in.

EVERYTHING THAT YOU SUSPECT IS TRUE

An Anjou pear is ripening on the sill,
there within your reach,
but you walk downstairs,
your palms rubbing the banister,
looking nowhere but ahead.

After we lift your boxes of books
and clothes to the cab,
the snow stiffening against the cold,
candid in the dark,
I have nothing to say.
To ask you to stay
is to stand in the full length of a mirror
revealing everything that you suspect is true.

Ping-pong and scotch in the pavilion
until 3 A.M.
The lilt of two voices
volleying across a net
has finally collapsed: our paddles hurled down.
Riding to the airport
we sit in the backseat holding hands,
not holding onto anything more.

When my body reaches back
later that night
into a rocking chair's safety,
I'm remembering the last time
you watched me button my blouse,
pull my sweater on over my head,
watching me close you out.

You hand me my Egyptian earring,
its face the face of Nefertiti
lifted over the dead.
You give me nothing
that is not already mine,
even the freezing rain
I walk home in
after waking early
to mail a letter to you
that comes back marked "Insufficient Postage."
Rain falls from these hemlocks
a Norwegian landscaper has spaced too close together,
rain falling nowhere but outside this house,
on this bare earth.

GHOST TOWN

For two months I've been analyzing your
letter, its air no longer brisk, grass green
or azaleas flaming. The swimming pool
sheeted with tarp, the billiard cues busted,
this place is a ghost town where the rowboat lies
capsized, stopped dead on the pier.
If cordiality's dour, the air chokes
with decay. The leaves my neighbors burn
rustle in wind moving through my bones.

BECAUSE OF THAT

The heat rose
from the jittery wood-burning stove
to the stifling loft.
We squeezed into a single cot
beneath the window blocked with ice.
We should have smashed it open.
Then that gush of wind, the world,
could have pushed through the glass
with comfort or miracles.

You did not say you were bored.
Saturday morning you hiked to town
for Sunday's paper.
The heavy clink of the milk jug
you toppled over in the dark
did not startle me from sleep.

Now I am miles away
from those backwoods where I lost you.
To have remained aloft, held there
in each other's arms
like planks pressed with kindling
until they caught!

You slept during the night-long drive
to the cabin,
in the twenty-below frost,

49

past the mountains gutted with coal.
Driving through the Allegheny tunnel
tucked inside that hollow,
I did not suspect quietness
among our errors.

COUPLE HELD AT A DISTANCE

They are out there, a chance
sighting, the tide rushing
forward, inching back.
If the waves held a lobster boat and a couple
much older, mending a net, there would be no need
to explain why I see us struggling.
If I still spoke with you maybe
once or twice a year,
I would ask first off, if you ever bury
your legs in the sand
and, sliding into its avalanche, remember
waving to me from the other side of the kiosk.
You were leaning into a chair
talking with someone I did not recognize,
smiling while she said something.
I used to think I would find you everywhere,
sun in my eyes. Now thinking I see you
is a distraction, the sea rising up in jets,
halfway to a dream.
The sea does not stop. Does not end.
The pain does not end. In fact the horseshoe crabs lying
dead on the sand all the way to the bird sanctuary
have migrated here for ages.

FIRE

After closing time
we tail a siren
to a hotel on 43rd
where one side of the building is peeled back
in a zigzag of red
smoke and flames.
A fire-escape door opens
three flights up
and a woman with waist-length gray hair
falls out exhaustedly.

I can see how our dancing earlier
is a mirror image of our despair
over the woman we do not know
how to save.
On the dance floor we held each other
gliding and turning
toward the front
door of the club
as if mesmerized by the darkness.

I can give you up
but it is harder
to stay with you and not feel
trapped by the slant edge of the bed
and the incense smoldering
on the table.
There they are: the firemen at the door
with ropes and pickaxes raised
to break through
the locked doors of the sleepers.

They will drag them mercilessly
downstairs, leave them
on the sidewalk
in the cold
where we look at each other
as into a fire
purging everything it touches.

3

She looked up over her knitting and met the third stroke and it
seemed to her like her own eyes, searching as she alone could
search into her mind and her heart, purifying out of existence
that lie, any lie . . .

—Virginia Woolf

To the Lighthouse

SUSTENANCE

for Saley Nong and Ed Dinger

In a wood made shadowy and uncertain
by mist, every step a loosening
of mulch and leaves, black
molding trunks driving me farther uphill,
I dreamed of sleeping on a tombstone in rain,
in a camp without tents, without meat,
with rice cut with stones, pebbles

that shine in the cesspool for a moment.
Saley told me about all that unattainable
pleasure flowering in the pool's skillet,
a taste for salt dug by hand from the earth.
I corrected her papers, adding the words:
carrion, stench, lice, charred,

but I brushed past her desk each morning
in leather boots, denim skirt, the usual
manufactured clothes I wore, with clean hair,
polished nails and three rings.
At a party once, a woman turned toward me
saying she deserved to be killed
for keeping servants, a villa,

a sea-coast apartment, sheepskins and bracelets,
for not giving them over to the poor
of her country. As an American, she said,
you can understand this kind of greed.
I knew Saley and Neneng polished eggs
they stole from the cafeteria for gifts,

and I knew women born in this country
who gave more, or less, cheaply, for love.
I thought of the compositions she wrote,
assignments in description: the hard
rap of sugarcane against a man's head;
the clearing the length of his body;
the swollen corpse weeks of rain washed up,

when she met her parents for a picnic
at the lake, then found herself in a boat
on the open sea, fleeing her country.
In my dream, someone was working a cigarette
in his mouth, then brushed my cheek
with one clove-scented lip. When I woke,
the bitter taste of clove still burned

n my throat, as it must have burned
n Saley's throat. It stayed with me
hrough the long curl and glare of an afternoon,
hen disappeared by early evening,—
reen kelp no longer illuminating the water,
he basket of yams and figs, the wild
unshot and chatter.

FRENCH MOVIE

for Ron Fein

A man rows out in a rubber dinghy to rescue his son's sailboat. It's a motorized toy the French make. This looks like a scene in a French movie, a farce about lovers caught in a triangle. Years later, the boy will play it back in his head. Here, the triangle's between the man, the dingy, and the motorized sailboat. The relationship between the man and the dinghy is clear. It's keeping him buoyant. The relationship between the man and sailboat is muddy. He's bought it for his son, no, someone else has. The man is separated from the boy's mother and only sees him on Sundays, living the other days of the week in some sort of hell. His wife's boyfriend bought the boat, which makes the boy's father feel like hell and wish the boat would sink. He's got to show his son he cares enough to try and save it, though a pact is already worked out in his head to let the boat go down, like the wink Zeus gives Hades when he asks for Persephone back. Then Hades knows it's alright to take her by force. The man's accustomed to putting on a show, first with his wife, then with his son, and now with his son's boat. The show is the variable that is constant in the man's relation-ships. The son's old enough to realize he'll never get his boat back. He's stopped trusting his father. The pond is like the world they shared and it's also the father's passage back to Hell. Everything would have been different if they'd been sailing for real, moving with the wind. Now the man's trying to lasso the sailboat with an oar. There are people watching, but when the rain begins, and the pond rings and rings, the people run off. The boy stays and watches. The pond does all the boy's crying.

WHAT STOPPED HER

What stopped her from going back to pick up the doll
she dropped getting out of the car was my interest
in what she was doing, an adult's interest,
something she sensed. I watched out of curiosity
not concern. Was she waiting for me to hand her the doll,
her arms already full with ballet shoes,
tiara, a stack of picture books, and nothing in mine?
She was too blonde. Her hair held all the sun.
She left her doll on the road in the twigs
and chicken bones and walked the flagstone
wiggling her fanny. She knew I was watching.
When would she go back for it? Would she wait
until I left, or until she missed it? I go back
when I am torn with regret, like the trip to Maine
last summer, watching the sag of lobster boats
through binoculars, as if to magnify each wave's swell
before it crashed. The tide goes out in an hour.
There is not a single boat in the harbor. The logical conclusion is
she's outgrown it, but we don't know that
when something slips from our grasp.

IN GRANDFATHER'S STAMP ROOM

On his desk lay the magnifying glass.
The bookcases cragged with catalogs,
tweezers, rice-paper envelopes.
I pressed the metal rim against my eye
and entered the momentarily cold world
of the pince-nez: Catherine II

mounted on dark-violet, violent champion
of the Romanoff dynasty's cultrated series;
bemused, unshaven, Grandfather seemed as fugitive
in his nursemaid's capacity
as Duchessa di Galliera's illegitimate son
and heir, Phillip Ferrary,

maniacal philatelist, vagabonding Europe
scavenging country attics
in pursuit of the Hawaii 2-cent blue.
After Grandmother's first stomach spasms,
Grandfather began to invest in stamps,
a steelworker's salary dross,
the vault in his study installed

when his three children rushed back
from their foster homes
after Grandmother's year-long trial
with diabetes. The Third Reich
found a place in his collection,
more than twenty pale-pink silhouettes

of the Fuhrer, LZ-192 Hindenburg bombers
facing a row of watermarked
bicolored child buglers. When I turned thirteen
Grandmother was recuperating
from her thirtieth operation.
She coaxed me into her bedroom
with chewing gum and exposed

her scarred body,
punctured stitch wounds, red-orange serrations,
dull-yellow bruises and alizarin blood-clot
points of intersection.
In hundreds of case studies,
classified the exception
she planned to overdose on barbiturates

while Grandfather mooned over the unattainable
1-franc, orange-vermilion
head of the goddess Ceres
and proofread his introductory letter
announcing "Joe's Stamp Exchange."
My grandfather found his stamp books' omissions
more urgent than life's.

PINPOINTS OF STARS

On the way to school
two girls sitting
across from me laugh
when a gang of boys
race from car
to car.

They flash by
with the terrifying
gleam of their knives
in their hands, sharp
pinpoints of fear lit up
like stars.

I want to ask
how they can laugh
when I don't dare.
I don't want those boys
noticing
anything about me.

One girl's gold
tooth brands her
flesh with poor
dentistry. I overhear,
*Eugene can't help falling
asleep on me. He's so tired at night.*

65

Her friend shakes her head,
laughs again
exposing no gold,
no bridge
to dangle our feet over
when she sees me staring.

THROWN OUT

Years ago my father threw me out.
It happened when he stopped mentioning the heat,
the smell of sour yams
and the mud caked on the floor.
It happened when he found out
nothing can be covered up,
a bad odor fills every room in a house.
It happened when the windows were closed in the evening
for locusts
and neighbors who watch for the daughter
running past shops,
past the last house in town,
its stone facade fallen to the street in shingles,
past acres of melon
to the channel,
that place of danger,
where hundreds of cuttlefish drown each season,
where Father forbade me to go
those stark afternoons I sat
poking a cuttlefish with a stick,
those evenings I circled the bank
waiting for the shrimp boy,
for his cap on my head,

for his voice of no anger,
our heads thrown back,
our eyes closed to the open threat
because we wanted to know by heart
breakers becoming witlessly, in that moment, still.

TWINS

Because I was rolling tobacco on the bank,
because I was sipping whiskey
when the train rushed against the scrub pines
only one of us stumbled on the tracks.
There was the forced clang
of iron braking.
There was the piston's lifted blade.

That night I stayed awake
watching the tiered flames of the oil refinery
across the river
flicker and converge into one body
and though the air outside was not redolent,
the flame spread outward igniting each bare branch.

There were stories of girls our age
dressing up in heels,
falling asleep in someone's arms beneath the pier.
For weeks I dreamed
of snow rising to the windows,
as I lay feverish beneath a mound of quilts.

That morning my friend and I had bathed in a creek.
We held nets of honeysuckle
in our palms, carried their scent to the tracks
where a soft-reddish glow from the refinery
streaks the sky
and smoke thins out across the horizon
locking a long row of houses.

ISTORY OF MY WORLD

m still as lost as I was in those days,
tchhiking on the Schuylkill with Linda.
arly fall, leaves severed from their clinging,
 we walked the roaring
eadow of roadway above the river
 the rush of cars yielding
nly to disappear at full throttle.

as it from the smoldering tip of a cigarette
eld out the window of a blue VW
verving into a serpentine,
e pony-tailed driver cast gold in daylight,
at I construed the syllables of my name,
e way the miller's daughter heard the wind,
e trees, the reeds along the edges
 the lake whispering *Rumpelstilskin*,
fering her the knowledge to reclaim

e child she conceived? It's really me,
ho I am, I want to discover, spinning
raw into gold, with the help of Linda,
hose fingers hold out the clove-scented cigarettes
e presses to my lips. I remember watching
er walk right up to a boy she didn't know
d put her hands under his shirt, and when
e moved the hair off his neck, kissed him there,

I knew that I wanted him to touch me.
It's hazy now, but I remember later
that day holding a hand of gin rummy,
not a single match. Linda upstairs.
One of the guys coming down and asking,
"Do you know how to wiggle your tits like your friend?"
I didn't answer—the hearts and diamonds roused
in my hands like the cars rushing past
on the highway where I walked with her,

so that the air whooshes into tunnels
of sound, even words that are shouted.
Fixated on the cards in my hand, afraid
of what would come next if I stood up
and watched them slip into some new striving,
I don't think I realized then that this was
the hand dealt out to me, the form my life
was taking—random and incoherent,

as Linda called my name from upstairs
and I pretended not to hear. I don't
remember what time it was when we finally left,
late enough to be reminded of a punishment,
but she was the emergence I was drawing
into me, pushing through the fence of hemlocks
in our yard, the scratchy branches grown so close
together, each limb inextricably part
of the future of the body beside it.

FREDERICK HARDING

Frederick Harding hears telegraph wires hum
    Like nerves the mind's exposed
And thinks: here are the notes for the truest score
    Anyone's ever composed.

Armed with pencils and pads he paces
    His room, counting
The lies he hears, sweet and clear,
    In a nightingale's song.

He comes to dinner unshaven.
    His jacket's a yellow filament,
As if daylight never flooded the sky
    And night spun in his head

Night is a record he plays and plays,
    Mists gathering, horses neighing,
Barns blazing, burned to the ground
    Every word ever learned.

Distracted from sleep, he strolls by the pool
    One night the full moon
Shines bright in its orbit, and coeds
    Buck-bathe there alone.

His head in the bushes, he stares and stares.
　　　They yell, *Go away, go away,*
Or we'll call the police. You're obscene.
　　　Go away. Get lost.

The dream of a nightwalker, a thousand feet up,
　　　Scanning the pinkish valley,
Its flesh, flesh, flesh, eyes and hair
　　　Hardish stays and stares.

Noting the stress and counter stress
　　　Of wind lashing, the cedar's moan
In his head, breathless, thin of air
　　　Walking the water's edge.

XTREMES

To keep the neighbors wondering, your parents anxious,
you don't need to do much, though one girlfriend
used to sneak out through her bedroom window
while her parents were sleeping, or open it wide
to let a friend climb in. She cut her wrist
on the glass once returning. Without waking
her parents, she lay unconscious all night
beneath a blue hedge. My sister, too,
often climbed out her window over the garage,
she climbed down by jumping onto a bench
dragged out the night before. She knew Mother
was not a somnambulist and took advantage
of her dedication to sleep. We chose
our own clothes and served ourselves breakfast,
light brimming the window. Mother was watching
when my sister drove up on the lawn just in fun,
then struck down the birches—saplings just planted,
spun off the lawn, circling our street's dead end.

LYSSA

Mother locked me in the shed. Nightmares. Locusts.
I banged on the door, *Mother, where are you?*
Where was her conscience? We walked the railroad's
gully. Mother rubbed my lips with whiskey,
wouldn't say how much farther or why we'd come
to such a difficult place: turkey hawks, mice,
thistle. On the track she's taken me, the sky
is gunmetal, the earth iron and rust, my heart
a red light flashing. She left me with the revivalists.
They dragged me to the altar, poured water
in my hands, said *Drink, young'un, drink.*
Slake your thirst in God. My lips kept moving.
Suddenly I was singing the words to their songs.
They rose in me like a thicket spiking the horizon.
I was happy. The children played with my hair,
weaved braids, weaved a halo of coppery leaves.
We played saint's statues standing knee deep
in morning glories. But one night I woke
to wailing, Mother staggering on the steps,
her face chalk white, calling *Lyssa. Lyssa.*
Wheat blazing. Horses neighing. Everything important
happens in imagination: Mother waking heat-cracked
as mud, unable to speak or rise. Have I mentioned
mother's glade? Dry stalks, crimson leaves, ducks lifting

and leaning, suspended in pure air. You crane
your neck to watch them and for the moment
time stops. Wind booms in the trees. The flock corkscrews upward.

Nothing ever ends, but it stays inside you.

WHITE SAIL

for Federico Fraguad.

I don't know what it would mean
if I one day stopped seeing a white sail
in the distance, if I looked out
across the river and saw nothing
as deliberate and solitary as a sail
raised to the wind. Even people
who sit directly across from you,
across a table, sometimes dream a sail inside them
and live loftily. You, lying next to me,
saying, *dame un beso,* in Spanish, your language.
We're lounging on chaises
rented for the hour
on the top deck of a dayliner
up the Hudson, the cold air
all around us, the river simply gray.
I remember being someone else, walking home
to my apartment then, one small room
and a window facing a neighbor's,
some apples ripening on her sill,
forever out of reach,
walking home in snow that touches
the backs of my legs, my knees,
wondering how deep things need to fall
before they stop,
just as I wonder now looking up at cliffs,
bridges, people playing cards,

um and cokes splashing into paper cups,
or listening to a man in polka-dotted bathing trunks
explain how he lost
his front teeth during a boxing match
when he was hit in the elbow,
his body oiled with suntan lotion
as if he were even now standing in the ring
preparing for a fight
against himself. You offer me
a sip of wine from your glass, but just then
the boat's mooring at West Point,
stalling to a stop. Wine spills on my skirt.
The man who was once a boxer hands me a napkin.
You watch me take it,
pretending you are the referee
shouting one . . . two . . . three . . .
long after the cloth's been cleaned
testing how determined I am
to keep something from becoming ruined.

ARGUMENTUM AD HOMINEM

Could merely changing seats one morning,
my hands groping for the surface
after each turn of the wheel
your hands usually float
so calmly upon, make us realize
how much our fingers interlocking
into a perfect dovetail hurt
at the joints? I see us
sitting beside one another arguing
over what to do
about the hole in the crotch
of my dance tights, double-parked
beside Claes Oldenburg's "Clothespin,"
two naked wooden bodies
clasped together in an everlasting
embrace on Market Street.
I want to see you
as the old you sliding your flaming
hands into place between my legs,
like a traveler
intuiting the right direction,
so much in love,
you then wield a map describing how
to build a dancewear shop
across the street, conjure up
an entire monument in the time it takes to turn
to see it. And there I was sliding off

the edge of something too high up
to be my seat. Like a doused sail,
my lips were clamped shut,
unwilling to pass even a word
between us. You: what were your desires
outside the lie of being late for work?
Did you really expect me
to drive you there first, then go home
and rummage through all our drawers for another pair
of tights I would not be able to find?
Once, I waited for you
at the finish line of a marathon
forgetting what time you told me
you expected to cross the line,
but when the 12-seconders came in
and you still had not, I panicked and rushed
unseen to the medics. The hour I waited never thinking
anything could have gone wrong
then seeing your arms
double-threaded with tubes
running into breakable bottles,
I realized how far
apart from you I had come
to stand. Every tall
man with a runner's number
tied around his chest
was stamped with your image.
Each time someone crossed
the line I did a double-take

not to see you,
and when I could not find you,
I felt as pained as if I had lost myself,
as if you were only an idea
I had grown in my heart,
childishly searched out,
and there among the multitude
of racers pounding down leg after leg
repeatedly missed. I see you
getting out of the car, yanking your briefcase
free of the seat, struggling not to leave
it behind you, thinking
what happened should not be forgotten.
Clutched tightly, it is the work it takes
to find what is true in us.

LABRADOR

When will the eighty-foot iceberg
float in the Labrador
of your heart finally break up
and you stop dragging me,
blindfolded, down the one
available access road
to that darkest region?

Shaking, suckled on two cups
of morning expresso, I shoved
a quarter into the slot
and counted ten metallic trills
until you, wiping shower
water from your eyes, finally
picked up, and I stammered out
that our new gold van, only
three days out from the dealer's,
had just been hit
from behind and that the guy
who did it said he had merely looked
away. I never dreamed
you would not ever believe me,
that you would not take on faith
anything I had to say,
when our yet unmade bed
still held the impression
of angel's wings, our joined arms
guttering against the sheets.

But when you insisted,
"Is that the true story?"
I had really heard your words
and the truth they were able to pin down
about us. The reaction I felt
is what happens to me at the optometrist's
when the technician holds open
my lids and squirts drops
in my eyes. My vision goes
so blurry I can't tell which is the mirrored
part of the wall and lose track of where
I depend on seeing myself;
the large green type on the cover
of *National Geographic* grows
as windswept as prairie grass
that, undisturbed for a century,
once drew bison.
Within a week you started
asking me what the date was of the accident,
and when you said the word "accident,"
you drew in a rod
to reel out of the fiercer sea
of me some big submerged lie,
the grappling hook still in.
I would say "Fuck you,"
if I thought that could do it,
but I ache to have you believe me.

NOTES

"I Begin to Leave Home When I Read Darwin" was inspired by my reading of Alan Moorehead's *Darwin and the Beagle*. The italicized portions of this poem are direct quotations from Darwin's diaries as they appear in Moorehead's book.

Lines 6 through 10 in "The Magnitude of the Crisis" were written by Cheryl Levin.

The italicized portions in "Looking at the Temple of Dendur" are actual segments from papers composed by my students in a course entitled "Writing from Life Experience" at The College of New Rochelle, South Bronx Campus.